Hello/Goodbye

Peter Souter

SERVING THEATRE

S F

SINCE 1830

SAMUELFRENCH-LONDON.CO.UK
SAMUELFRENCH.COM

Author's note

Some thanks.

Anthony, for not firing me as a client despite not making much commission.

Nicki, for getting this published.

Gordon, for getting bits of Act Two broadcast on Radio 4.

Richard, for teaching me how to write. Kind of.

Renu, for fixing my appalling spelling and grammar.

Sheila & Brian, for the initial conception.

Maggie, for being married to me for a really long time.

It's much easier to write about love when you are in love.

Peter Souter

Hello/Goodbye was first performed at Hampstead Theatre, Downstairs on 1 March 2013. The cast was as follows:

Juliet   Jo Herbert
Alex   Andy Rush
Leo   Leo Staar
Amanda   Yolanda Kettle

Director   Tamara Harvey
Designer   Lucy Osborne
Lighting   David Holmes
Composer   George Dennis

Revived at Hampstead Theatre, Upstairs on 21 January 2015 with the following cast:

Juliet   Miranda Raison
Alex   Shaun Evans
Leo   Luke Neal
Amanda   Bathsheba Piepe

Director   Tamara Harvey
Designer   Lucy Osborne
Lighting   David Holmes
Sound   Emma Laxton
Composer   Jared Zeus

To Maggie

CHARACTERS

JULIET
ALEX
LEO
AMANDA

ACT ONE

Int. The flat. Day.

*A good looking, if slightly odd young man moves
cardboard packing boxes around a shabby kitchen.
He's moving in.*

*After a few moments of this we hear the front
door opening and the sound of high heeled shoes
approaching. A young woman with beautiful, fire-red
hair stomps into the kitchen holding a box of pans in
one hand and a McDonald's Happy Meal in the other.*

*When she spots the young man she drops the pan box
with a clang and begins to shout at him, with a force
that is at odds with her slender frame.*

JULIET Who the freezing fuck are you?

ALEX I'm Alex.

JULIET I don't mean your name! I don't care about your
name! I mean who the fucking fuck are you and why are
you in my flat?!

ALEX I'm not.

JULIET I can see you! There! If you're a- a- a figment of my
imagination why is there an overpowering smell of sweat
in here??

ALEX *(slightly flustered by her beauty)* The sweat is from the boxes. Well from me obviously but caused by the boxes. The lifting of said. They're heavy. On account of the stuff. Inside them. And it's a hot day. Ergo. Sweat.

> JULIET *calms a little, seeing she's in no danger from this odd boy. Switching from fear to mockery in an instant.*

JULIET Who the hell says 'ergo'? Whilst breaking into someone's flat? What kind of a person does that?

ALEX I'm not breaking in. This is my flat. I live here. As of today.

JULIET No half-wit. This is my flat. I live-here-as-of-today.

> JULIET *'s obviously spikey nature helps* ALEX *get over the discombobulating power of her beauty.*

ALEX Well.

JULIET Well?

ALEX Well. There's been a mix up. Clearly.

JULIET Yathink?

ALEX Yes. You, a shouty woman with slightly disastrous hair, have been misinformed. About my flat.

> JULIET *smooths down a corner of her wild hair.*

JULIET Stay there. Don't take any more of your crap out of any more of your boxes while I… Call the estate agent and/or arrange for my enormous boyfriend to come round and beat the squits out of you…

> *She fumbles a large, late 90's mobile out of her bag and stomps into the hall.* ALEX *stands perfectly still for a*

*moment. Then he wanders over to the Happy Meal bag
that* **JULIET** *has dumped on the counter and pokes a
finger inside so he can examine its contents.*

*After a long moment he takes a small green dinosaur
toy from inside the McDonald's bag. He slides it from
the wrapper and winds it up methodically.*

*The toy totters along the counter before committing
suicide into his waiting hand at the other end.*

JULIET *stomps in and out while this is happening.*

JULIET *(on the phone)* … 15A Peach St… Peach! Like the
fruit! … What do you mean "you see the problem"? …
What??? … Are you some kind of mental deficient? …
Are you part of an outreach programme? Morons in the
community? … Why should that matter to me? … So? … I
don't care if there are two agents… You are my agent and
I need you to come round here immediately and have this
man removed…

> **JULIET** *exits. Finding himself alone* **ALEX** *rewinds the
> little dino, lies on the floor and lets it climb across his body
> like it is rough terrain.*

JULIET *(off)* … I sent you a cheque! … What does it
matter who was first?!? … The door was open!

> **JULIET** *stomps through on her second circuit.*

JULIET Hold on… *(to* **ALEX***)* … Are you dead? Don't die
in my flat. Die by all means but go out into the garden
first… *(to the agent)* No, not you… Well, you too actually…

> *She exits again, rage keeping her on the move. The
> dinosaur grinds to a halt just as it is about to topple
> into* **ALEX***'s mouth. He gets up, carefully places it back
> into its original packaging and sets it gently on the*

work top. **JULIET** *stomps back into the kitchen.*

JULIET *(to the agent)* ... But before you die sort out this shit!

> *Unable to express her incandescence properly she tries to hang up by stabbing the phone buttons randomly with her finger. Then, boiling over, she suddenly snaps it in two with surprising strength.*

> *Immediately remorseful she tries to jam the flip-out mouthpiece back in place. When the attempt fails she loons out all over again. Apoplectic, she hurls the pieces into a bucket of water that stands by the sink with a mop sticking out.*

> *The whole event starts out comic. But then, somewhere in the middle, it becomes faintly frightening. This girl has a lot going on.*

> *A long beat. Then* **ALEX**, *an oddish boy himself, takes an unexpected tack...*

ALEX Can I have this?

JULIET What?

ALEX Can I have this?

JULIET The toy?

ALEX Yes.

JULIET The toy dinosaur?

ALEX Yes please.

> *Oddly,* **JULIET** *calms a little.*

JULIET Why would a grown man want a green plastic T-Rex?

ALEX You're the one eating the Happy Meal.

JULIET I like Happy Meals. I'm a happy person. And, P.S., get-out-of-my-flat!

ALEX Sounded to me like your estate agent thinks it is my flat.

JULIET My estate agent is a dead man. It's just a question of pecking order now. First you, then him? Or him then you? I can't decide.

ALEX It's a Stegosaurus by the way.

JULIET What now?

ALEX A Stegosaurus. Not a T-Rex. Little plates on its back, see. A clue.

JULIET Why do you want it?

ALEX I collect them.

JULIET T-Rexes?

ALEX Again, it's a…

JULIET I know what it is. It's a piece of cheap green crap designed to trick children into eating cheap brown crap smothered in cheap red crap. Who collects that?

ALEX I have… every toy McDonalds have ever given away with a Happy Meal.

He scoops an old wooden type case from one of his packing cases. Each little box in the case has a

> *colourful, cheap toy carefully displayed in it. There are*
> *dozens of similar cases in the box. Seeing* **JULIET** *has no*
> *interest he puts it back and picks up the little dinosaur.*

ALEX This one is new and I don't have it yet. You'd be saving me from buying the meal. Which I never actually eat. Not a big fan of…

JULIET Cheap-brown-crap-smothered-in-cheap-red-crap.

ALEX Exactly.

JULIET Sure.

> **JULIET** *switches tack, deciding to play a little with this*
> *idiosyncratic and not unattractive boy.*

ALEX Sure what?

JULIET Sure you can have it.

ALEX Oh. Thanks.

JULIET *(light)* If you get out of my flat. Immediately. Then the stegorexasaur is all yours.

ALEX *(with a hint of Aspergers)* That's not a great deal. This is a nice flat. I like my flat. I'll just go buy myself a Happy Meal and keep on living here if it's all the same to you.

JULIET What if it's the last one?

ALEX How do you mean?

JULIET What if I've got the last one. What if you've been collecting all this time and now you're going to miss one and the whole thing will be ruined?

ALEX Shut up.

JULIET Shut up?

ALEX Shut up.

She's greatly cheered by uncovering his weak spot.

JULIET Did I hit a nerve? Did I hack right into the core of your inner being? Did I now?

ALEX I do actually have kind of a... phobia about that sort of thing.

JULIET Ha! I knew it!

She walks over to the sink and clicks on the waste disposal, which gurgles into grinding activity. Then she holds the dinosaur over the plug hole.

JULIET Move out or the fossil cops it.

ALEX You really ought to run the water.

JULIET What?

ALEX If you've got the waste disposal on you're supposed to have the water running. Otherwise you can damage the motor. My motor.

JULIET *(enjoying herself now)* Not as much as myyyy motor will damage your precious plastic crapasaurus.

ALEX There'll be others.

JULIET How can you be sure?

ALEX McDonalds is the world's largest toy manufacturer.

JULIET Rubbish. They make hot cow sludge.

ALEX Largest by miles. Three times bigger than Toys "R" Us. Who are the next biggest.

JULIET How do you know all this stuff? Waste disposals, toy stats. Are you one of those Rain Men?

ALEX You've lost me.

JULIET Rain Man! *(like Dustin Hoffman)* "I'm an excellent driver".

ALEX You are an unusual person...

He seems to be reaching for her name and, to **JULIET**'s *slight surprise, she supplies it.*

JULIET Juliet.

ALEX You are an unusual person, Juliet.

JULIET Thanks.

ALEX Not altogether sure it was a compliment.

JULIET I'll live with the disappointment. *(cheery)* You, on the other hand, are a certified freak.

ALEX Not much ambiguity there.

JULIET Nope.

A beat. **ALEX** *is still focused on getting the Stegosaurus.*

ALEX Why did the dinosaur cross the road?

JULIET Don't know. Or care.

ALEX Because they didn't have chickens in them days.

JULIET Jesus!

She laughs though. Then she stares at **ALEX**. *Scanning and appraising.*

JULIET Is it me or is it really hot in here?

She tugs open the top two buttons of her denim shirt.

ALEX It's not you. Summertime. Hot everywhere.

JULIET It seems particularly hot in my flat.

ALEX Or my flat as its known in legal circles. Want me to open a window?

JULIET No.

ALEX Would you like a cup of tea?

JULIET I only drink coffee.

ALEX Figures.

JULIET What's that supposed to mean?

ALEX You seem wound up. Unusual and wound up. Unusually wound up.

JULIET I'm always tetchy when my estate agent turns out to be an incompetent two-timing dullard and I've nowhere to sleep tonight.

ALEX Don't you have friends?

JULIET Hundreds.

ALEX Why don't you sleep with one of them?

JULIET All my friends hate me.

ALEX Wow. Never saw that coming.

JULIET Hey! They all loved me until I… accidentally tripped and fell on top of one of them.

ALEX Were they badly hurt?

JULIET I had sex with him, fool.

ALEX Oh. Aaaand that caused ill feeling amongst your wide community of friends because…?

JULIET He'd just got married to one of my other friends. That afternoon as it happens.

ALEX Yes. I can see how that would cause a commotion.

JULIET So I had to get out of Dodge. Found a flat, this one, wrote a cheque and lived happily ever after. In theory.

ALEX How's that theory working out for you?

JULIET Don't get cocky. This isn't over. They're working on it. They're going to call me back.

> **ALEX** *looks down at the water bucket, gently tips it over with his toe spilling out a little puddle of water. The mobile phone lies in its centre.*

JULIET Bollocks.

ALEX Well, quite.

JULIET Okay. Okay. This is getting serious now. Are you saying you won't move out of my flat?

ALEX No. I'm afraid not.

JULIET Even though I asked you nicely?

ALEX When did you do that?

JULIET Even though I tried to reason with you?

ALEX Again, when did you...

JULIET Right! You leave me no choice! I'm going to have to-to-to have my boyfriend come over and squish your head.

ALEX How was he about the whole sleeping with the groom extravaganza, incidentally?

JULIET He'll get over it.

ALEX He'll squish my head for ruthlessly moving into my own flat but he's squeamish about squishing your recently married sex friend's head?

JULIET He does what he's told.

ALEX Sounds like an idyllic love match you've got going there, Juliet.

JULIET I told you my name. I didn't give you permission to use it all the time.

ALEX Sugar?

JULIET No patronising nicknames either.

ALEX Do you want sugar? In your coffee.

JULIET Oh. No. *(highly ironic)* I'm sweet enough.

ALEX Clearly.

*Despite the threat of cartoon violence they begin to
settle into a rhythm of cheery verbal combat, like they've
watched one too many Hepburn and Tracy movies.*

JULIET Don't judge me on today. I'm delightful when I'm
not having my flat stolen.

ALEX Or bonking someone's recently acquired husband
presumably?

JULIET It's 2001, who the hell says bonking? Or
presumably for that matter.

ALEX Why can't you sleep at your amenable boyfriend's
house tonight?

JULIET We're not talking at the moment.

ALEX How were you going to communicate to him that
my head was in urgent need of rearrangement?

JULIET Text.

They both look down at her still drowned phone.

JULIET *(quiet)* Bollocks. Big, hairy bollocks.

*He hands her a coffee, starting to like her despite the
situation.*

ALEX Can't you stay with your Mum and Dad?

JULIET Parents divorced. One dead, other dead to me.

ALEX Brothers or sisters?

JULIET Neither.

Suddenly everything makes sense to ALEX.

ALEX Aaah. You're an only child.

JULIET What's that supposed to mean?

ALEX It means your parents didn't have other children.

JULIET No, I meant what's "aah" supposed to mean?

ALEX It's short for "ah-ha".

JULIET "Ah-ha"?

> **ALEX** *realises he's in trouble but can't see a way out.*

ALEX "Ah-ha" as in "ah-ha, it all makes sense now".

JULIET And what, pray tell, makes sense now?

ALEX You're an only child. Only children think the world revolves around them. Then, when it doesn't, they… behave badly.

> **JULIET** *casually takes a large, cast-iron frying pan out of her solitary box of packing.*

ALEX *(Rain Manish approval)* Ooh, Le Creuset. A sturdily constructed pan brand.

JULIET You think I'm badly behaved?

ALEX No.

JULIET No?

ALEX No. I know you're badly behaved. I'm just regretting bringing it up. Which one is dead and which one is dead to you?

JULIET You keep trying to change the subject. First the pans, now my parents. Just how badly behaved do you think I am?

She's having fun now, swinging the frying pan casually.

JULIET Think I'm bash-your-brains-out-with-a-sturdily-constructed-frying-pan badly behaved? Perchance?

ALEX It's crossed my mind.

JULIET (*turning on a sixpence*) My Mum is the dead one.

ALEX How'd she die? Did your father kill her with a cooking implement?

JULIET Cigarettes. But Daddy helped by leaving when I was little.

ALEX Aah.

JULIET "When police questioned the killer as to her motive Stone said the victim kept saying "aah" in an annoying and patronising way. The crown prosecution service has decided not to press charges".

ALEX Sorry. But you do keep saying text book stuff.

JULIET Please tell me you're not a psychiatrist AND a flat thief.

ALEX No. I'm not a psychiatrist.

JULIET What are you then? Apart from a creepy toy collector.

ALEX Album sleeves.

JULIET Album-sleeves isn't a sentence. It's like saying 'booklet-socks'.

ALEX I design album sleeves. For small bands. Tiny ones in fact. Don't marry me for my money because I don't have any.

JULIET Darn. That was really all that was keeping me from popping the question.

ALEX Pity. You can sleep with your own husband without upsetting all your friends.

> **JULIET** *is puzzled to find herself half flirting with the object of her dissatisfaction.*

JULIET So... You're doomed then.

ALEX How so?

JULIET Album sleeves. People have stopped buying albums. Even the ones that do will just, what's the word? ... 'download' them soon enough. Sleeve art is the Dodo of the graphic design world, isn't it?

ALEX You say unsettling things. Even for an only child with abandonment issues.

JULIET You're welcome. Do you have eggs?

ALEX Eggs?

> *She begins to bustle around the stove.*

JULIET Eggs. Nature's chicken bum-bounty.

ALEX Oh. Yes. Somewhere. Why?

JULIET I have half a loaf of ciabatta bread and some

chilli oil. And an expensive frying pan. If you have eggs, together we can make fried egg sandwiches. Devilled egg sandwiches in fact.

ALEX Are you hungry?

JULIET Always.

> *She fires up a ring and fishes out the chilli oil.*

ALEX You only have one box.

JULIET I travel light.

> *A moment's calculation...*

ALEX All you could grab as your boyfriend threw you out?

JULIET As I stormed out.

ALEX Pre-emptive storm out?

JULIET *(busted)* Shut up and find the eggs.

ALEX Chilli oil, bread and a frying pan. Odd things to grab.

JULIET I lose focus when I'm angry. Besides I wanted to have a devilled fried egg sandwich in my new flat.

ALEX But you forgot to pack eggs. And make sure you actually had a flat.

JULIET I was confident that I could pick up some eggs along the way. Or someone with eggs.

> *This sentence sticks in the air a little.* **ALEX** *fumbles around in a box and produces some eggs.*

JULIET I'm always right about these things.

> *She holds her arm high and loops an extravagant drizzle of chilli oil through the air in an arc down into the pan. Then she cracks the eggs expertly into it with one hand at speed.*

> **ALEX** *watches her intently, working things out in his slightly autistic way.*

ALEX You don't have burns on your forearms.

JULIET You say some very odd things. Even for a curly haired cretin.

ALEX You cook like a professional. Even when it's just eggs. But you aren't a chef. No forearm burns.

JULIET Maybe I'm just really careful.

ALEX Maybe you've got a dream but you're too chicken to follow it.

> *He's right.*

JULIET Wrong. Who wants to be a cook when you can work in the city, take your wages home in a wheel barrow, eat in the fancy restaurant and treat the waiters like crap?

> *But she flicks the pan to flip the eggs with an expert flourish. Over the next few lines she roots out some cheese from* **ALEX**'s *food box, turns the toaster on its side and slides bread and cheese inside it creating a Jamie Oliver-style home made Breveller. All very casual and very slick.*

> **ALEX** *carries on unpacking, mumbling to himself.*

ALEX Abandoned/only child/frustrated chef/wage slave.

JULIET What are you doing there Rain Man?

ALEX Unpacking. In my lovely new flat.

JULIET Sounded like you were rounding up all the information you'd tricked out of me.

ALEX Not tricked. You are very forthcoming.

JULIET Why are you collecting information? Reckon this flat thing is going to end in court? Think you can sway a jury with character assassination?

ALEX I'm not sure flat contract disputes go up before a full jury that often. They tend to save them for the frying pan murders.

JULIET So why the list? Here…

She hands him a beautifully presented devilled egg sandwich.

ALEX Thanks… Sorry, I'm a lister. A filer. A collector. A… Man this is a fantastic sandwich!

JULIET I know.

ALEX No, I mean really. This is the most delicious thing I've ever tasted.

JULIET Good.

ALEX And you just conjured it up out of nothing.

JULIET Well, if the man who has stolen something dear to you is alert to a frying pan murder… I tend to switch to poisoning.

ALEX *stops mid chew. He decides that the sandwich*

*is too delicious to worry about the slight chance she's
serious.*

JULIET So... The McDonald's toy thing. You thinking of
turning pro with that?

ALEX What's your point?

JULIET My point is what's the point?

ALEX Why does there have to be a point?

JULIET Pointless answer.

Seeing he needs a better answer, **ALEX** *digs deep.*

ALEX I like to... complete things. Stuff. Things.

JULIET *(sweetly)* Aah, that sounds sad, lonely and
slightly perverted.

ALEX Well, you asked. I like to start something, start
collecting something... then carry on until I have a
complete collection. The things themselves don't matter
as much as having everything.

JULIET And has anybody ever offered to take your
virginity out of sheer pity?

ALEX I do pretty well for sex actually. Turns out, oddly
enough, I'm... very...

JULIET Very...?

*   **ALEX** *has flushed now, only encouraging* **JULIET**
    further.

JULIET Veeery...

ALEX Very… good.

> **JULIET**'s *turn to be surprised and slightly embarrassed.*

JULIET Very good?

ALEX At sex. I'm very, er… good. At it. At making it an, ahm… enjoyable experience. For both parties.

JULIET Oh.

> *Her turn to be distracted. And to start gathering information.*

JULIET What way are you 'good'?

ALEX Most men don't pay enough attention to detail, *(getting less embarrassed)* but I like my partner to… complete.

JULIET Oh.

ALEX Altruism. In bed. Is the key. I think.

JULIET Oh.

ALEX Yes. Most people are surprised. I don't seem the type. Which helps in a way. I think.

JULIET How did we get to this?

ALEX You asked me about my hobbies.

JULIET I regret it and very much want to take it back. Can we return to the important business of throwing you out of my flat?

ALEX There's a phone in the hall if you want to call your guy again.

JULIET Why can't you call your guy?

ALEX My guy is a girl. She's given me keys and helped me arrange to have the utility bills. Did your guy do any of those things?

JULIET No. We had an argument on the phone and switched to email.

ALEX Do you feel a pattern building here Juliet?

JULIET Stop using my name like we're pals. Everyone hates estate agents, it's practically the law. I suppose you gave yours the orgasm of her lifetime after she'd handed over the details of the gas and lekky.

She isn't serious but, when **ALEX** *says nothing, she realises she's hit the nail on the head.*

JULIET Oh bloody hell! That's cheating! You shagged my flat from right under my nose??

ALEX Attention to detail. That's why they call it completing.

JULIET That's buying not renting.

ALEX My utility bills say different.

JULIET I will use your phone actually. The phone! My phone! Oh sodbuggerfuck.

Properly cross again for the first time in a while she stomps out and **ALEX** *allows himself the tiniest smile. He hangs one of the trays full of toys on the kitchen wall and puts the green dinosaur in an empty compartment, trying it for size.* **JULIET**'s *slightly high pitched tone drifts into the hall.*

JULIET *(off)* ... Just come round and help me! ... You know, Peach Street! Near the Starbucks we got chucked out of... okay 'I' got chucked out of...

> **ALEX** *wipes a little sweat off his brow and peels off his lumberjack shirt. Underneath he is wearing a white vest. He looks pretty good for a skinny, scruffy kid. Cooler, he opens up another box and takes a neatly mounted frame of 1930s American Baseball Cards and loops it onto the same picture rail as the McDonalds toys. Neatly possessing the room in* **JULIET***'s absence, he's hanging a long black glass-fronted box full of Japanese tin robots when she returns.*

JULIET You'll just have to take those down again when Leo gets here.

ALEX Leo?

JULIET My enormous rugby playing, head squishing boyfriend.

ALEX Didn't you guys break up?

JULIET A technicality. He'll be here soon, your head will be, will be, will be squished and, and, and I'll have my flat back: everybody wins.

ALEX Okay, do you mind if I carry on? Just in case he doesn't show?

JULIET Yes! I do mind. And what do you mean 'in case he doesn't show'? He'll show. Then he'll... show you.

> **ALEX** *has two more large, interestingly framed little collections in his hands. One of pinned and labelled insects, the other a complete set of Coke and Pepsi bottle caps, 1890s to the present day.*

ALEX What's best over the fridge? Bugs or Coke bottles.

JULIET Not bugs… dammit! Neither. I mean neither. Put them back in the box before **LEO** comes and, you know, squishes your head.

ALEX Oh, I'm sure it won't come to that.

JULIET What are you going to do? Give him the best orgasm he's ever had?? Even though you don't seem like the type???

ALEX My guess is we'll have a coffee, go through the chain of events reasonably enough and then he'll take you home with him to talk over whether your infidelity is caused by your father leaving you as a toddler or your mother dying tragically young.

JULIET That settles it. Up to now I wasn't serious about the violence thingy. But now I'm, I'm, I'm having him rip your head clean off! And impale it on the end of the mop. Maybe I'll start a collection: 'Flat thieving idiots on sticks!'

The doorbell rings.

JULIET Ha! Leo!

ALEX That was quick.

JULIET The idea was that we live near to each other.

ALEX So he could keep an eye on you?

JULIET Yes! … No! So he could… come round and beat up interlopers.

ALEX I'd better let him in then. So he can get to work on me.

He goes out the kitchen door. **JULIET** *betrays a hint of concern, not really wanting fisticuffs. Or to see* **LEO**.

ALEX *(off)* Hi. I'm Alex.

LEO *(off)* Leo. Is Juliet Stone here?

ALEX *(off)* Yup. Come in.

The two men return. **LEO** *is indeed a large man. But he seems pretty mild with it. If a little pissed off.*

ALEX Would you like a coffee?

LEO Er. Yes. Please. White, two sugars if you have them.

JULIET "Yes?" "Please??" "White two sugars if you have them"??? I said come round here and, and, and beat the squits out of him while also squishing his head! Not ask him for a date.

ALEX Hungry? Juliet makes an excellent devilled egg sandwich.

LEO *(suspicion instantly aroused)* Does she now? I thought you two had just met?

JULIET Yes! That's better! Fly into a jealous rage! Beat him up, kick him out and throw his ridiculous American Baseball Card collection out after him.

LEO His what?

ALEX She means the stuff on the wall.

LEO clocks the card collection and is instantly a small boy himself.

LEO Oh wow! You've got Babe Ruth and everything.

ALEX You like baseball?

LEO Exchange year at Princeton. Became wildly enthusiastic about all those sports the Americans made up so they can be the best in the world at them. Baseball, basketball, American football.

ALEX *(enjoying himself)* If you're a Princeton man you must be a Giants fan?

LEO Went to every game my friend Caspar and I could lay… hands… on…

> *The name Caspar seems to remind him that* **JULIET** *is deeply in his bad books. He turns to her and tries to model his sweet natured face into a convincing storm.*

LEO Juliet, I think we need to talk.

JULIET Yes, yes, we can have a nice long chat when I've got my flat back.

LEO You can't just ring me up and ask me to beat up a complete stranger and not even mention you're sleeping with my best friend.

ALEX Ooh, you didn't mention the groom was Leo's best friend.

JULIET Detail.

LEO It wasn't a detail to me. It was humiliating.

ALEX *(mock concern)* I can see how it would be. I'm guessing Caspar?

LEO Who is this guy?

JULIET *(gentle, as if talking to a stupid child)* He's. The. One.

Who. Stole. My. Flat!

LEO You know you haven't even apologised.

JULIET Why should I apologise! He's living in my apartment!

ALEX I think he means the whole bonking the groom thing.

JULIET Shut up!

LEO Alex is right. I do mean that.

ALEX Told you. Here, hope it's not too hot.

LEO Thanks.

> *He hands the big man his coffee.* **LEO** *takes it daintily and drinks a sip.* **JULIET** *feels everything isn't going the way she'd hoped.*

JULIET Look. We'll do all that later. In private. Can't we just coax this guy out into the street where he belongs through the medium of violence and then sort out the other… stuff?

LEO I've got nothing against Alex. He seems a nice enough chap.

ALEX Why thanks Leo.

LEO Makes a decent cup of coffee.

ALEX *(having fun now)* The trick is not to press the plunger too early.

LEO As far as I know he hasn't slept with any of my close friends.

JULIET Don't be too sure. He's a sexual Olympian. According to him.

ALEX I wouldn't say Olympian. Maybe Commonwealth Games standard.

LEO I thought you were phoning to apologise.

JULIET I was. I just apologise better in the comfort of my own flat. I promise I'll get right to it when we're done with Alex.

ALEX Did they manage to patch things up?

LEO Who?

ALEX *(unable to resist)* Caspar and Mrs Caspar.

LEO No. They are going for a quickie annulment. Cheaper than a divorce.

News to **JULIET**. *Surprisingly it's surprising news to her.*

JULIET Oh. I didn't know.

ALEX Suppose you weren't high on the list of people they'd call.

LEO Who is this guy?

JULIET *(refocused)* He's an annoying, lonely git who designs album sleeves that nobody buys, collects McDonald's toys and mouldy cigarette cards, gives people surprise orgasms and moves into women's flats until their boyfriends throw him out.

ALEX Unless the woman in question is a volcanically bad tempered only child with Daddy issues who cheats on said boyfriend and therefore reduces his motivation.

LEO You two seem to know each other pretty well.

JULIET What?

LEO For people who are supposed to have only met 20 minutes ago. You seem pretty familiar. With each other.

JULIET What??

LEO Orgasms and mouldy cigarette cards and so on.

ALEX They aren't mouldy actually. I freeze dry them before I fra...

JULIET Will you be quiet and get on with the important business of banging your face against Leo's knuckles?

But **LEO** *has heard enough.*

LEO Thanks for the coffee Alex. Don't let her spend too much time with your best friend.

JULIET What???? You're leaving?

ALEX I think he's leaving.

At the door a clearly emotional **LEO** *seems to see their entire relationship flash before his eyes.*

LEO We talked about getting married. We talked about growing old together. Buying a clapboard house on the Norfolk coast and doing it up. Getting a fat black labrador...

JULIET Mr Huffington Tuffington.

LEO *(as if this should have been the clincher)* We named an as-yet-unbought dog.

JULIET We did.

LEO You didn't mention having sex with my friends on their wedding days.

JULIET One friend. Singular. Not a whole bunch.

But this is not as helpful as she'd hoped.

LEO I bought a box of your stuff. It's on the step.

He's gone.

JULIET Stuff? What stuff? Leo! I don't want a box of stuff… I haven't got anywhere to put it.

There's a long pause, punctuated by the sound of the door slamming and a car pulling away.

ALEX He seemed nice.

JULIET *slumps to the floor, fiddling absentmindedly with the little green dinosaur.*

JULIET He was nice.

ALEX Big guy. Glad he wasn't the violent type.

JULIET Yes. Nice. Big. Gentle, now I think about it.

ALEX Maybe a tad boring.

JULIET Very boring.

ALEX The groom was probably funnier.

JULIET He was actually.

ALEX Though perhaps lacking a bit of judgement.

JULIET It was a spur of the moment thing.

ALEX You did it for the first time on his wedding day?

JULIET Oh no, we'd been doing it for months. The wedding day thing was just a fond goodbye really. If we'd made it upstairs everything would probably have been all right.

ALEX Unlucky.

JULIET *(missing the irony)* Yeah. Is it me or is it getting hotter in here?

ALEX It's a hot day.

> **JULIET** *is undone. And much more likable for it.*

JULIET The thing is… I've got a bit of a temper.

ALEX *(gentle)* Really?

JULIET And I'm, you know, impetuous.

ALEX I was getting subtle signals.

JULIET I had a bumpy start in life. Shedding parents like confetti. If enough things you don't want to happen… happen… eventually, they make you worry about what will… happen. Next. And you… try to make different things happen. First.

ALEX That's clear. A very clear explanation. Of the circumstances.

JULIET I don't actually like causing all this trouble. It just seems to be what happens. If I get out of bed in the morning. Trouble. Happens.

It's a sweet, muddled speech. **ALEX** *is not immune.*

ALEX Give me the dinosaur and you can have the box room.

JULIET Huh?

ALEX For a few weeks. If you promise not to sleep with my best friend, like Leo said.

JULIET *starts to reassemble her feisty front.*

JULIET I doubt you have a best friend.

ALEX I am a bit of a lone wolf as it happens.

JULIET Fancy phrase for 'lonely git'.

ALEX Do you want the room or not?

JULIET No! I don't want the box room in my own flat!

ALEX Please yourself.

She thinks for a minute, assessing her situation.

JULIET I want the master bedroom.

ALEX No chance.

JULIET Give me the master bedroom, where are your manners?

ALEX Right next to yours it seems. In, in, in non-existent-land.

JULIET Embarrassingly lame comeback. That means

you're basically fine with the idea.

ALEX It does not! In fact I withdraw the box room offer. I was just feeling sorry for you because you're homeless and you had a tricky start in life and you recently split up with your boyfriend.

JULIET He's no loss really. 'Mr Huffington Tuffington' is a stupid name for a Black Lab.

ALEX Fair point. You still missed the boat on the room though.

JULIET No, on reflection, I think I'll take it. But I want the big bathroom. You're a boy so you only need a small one.

ALEX I've got a large collection of rare sea shells. So I'll need the big one.

JULIET You're so selfish! Biggest bedroom, biggest bathroom!

ALEX It's my flat. I'm throwing you a bone.

JULIET Keep your bone. I want the big bathroom or the deal's off.

ALEX The deal's already off! I called it off a minute ago because I didn't feel you appreciated the gesture enough.

JULIET I'm prepared to accept the box room for now because I'll probably be out a lot of the time. But I'll need a proper bathroom. I like to soak.

ALEX You like to soak?

JULIET With my hands on the edge of the bath so my finger tips don't end up looking like Yoda's testicles.

ALEX That won't happen because you don't live here. I withdraw my offer. Made, incidentally, in a weak moment that has now passed.

JULIET I don't mind if you keep your shells in there. I quite like shells. I can look at them while I soak. I like the way they curl around.

ALEX Fibonacci numbers.

JULIET You're doing it again.

ALEX Doing what?

JULIET Saying random things in the course of normal conversation. That's why you shouldn't live alone. You'll get even more odd.

ALEX It wasn't a random thing. The Fibonacci numbers are the reason for the pleasing curl in all shells.

JULIET You say more about that crap while I get my box from the doorstep.

ALEX *(to her retreating back)* You don't need to get your box because, as I said, I've retracted the box room offer!

But she's already on her way.

JULIET *(off)* What's a Fibonacci number when it's at home?

ALEX It's a beautiful mathematical formula found throughout nature. A sequence. 1, 2, 3, 5, 8, 13, 21 And so on. You add the last number to the one before to get the next one.

JULIET returns with a box full of random possessions which she starts to empty onto the kitchen counter absently.

JULIET What's that got to do with my nice soak with the shells?

ALEX If you plot the numbers out as squares they make a spiral. The spiral that's in all shells. And in other places. The layout of sunflower seeds for example.

JULIET I like sunflowers too. Must get some for my little room.

ALEX You haven't got a little room. You're too rude and bad tempered to have a room. I don't know what I was thinking.

JULIET How can numbers make a spiral? Show me.

> *A born teacher and enthusiast,* **ALEX** *can't help himself. He gets one of those 'remember to get milk' chalk boards out of one of his boxes, wipes away the last shopping list and begins to chalk neat boxes.*

ALEX The first box is one. The second is two. The third three. Then 5. Then 8. Then 13. Then 21. See?

JULIET I see a bunch of boxes.

ALEX Then you use the corners to plot the spiral. See.

> *He draws the Fibonacci spiral through the line formed by the boxes.*

JULIET Ooh! Pretty! Like a shell!

ALEX And sunflower seed heads.

JULIET Blimey. You actually know something interesting. I'll think of you when I'm having my long soaks.

ALEX Why do you have pink furry handcuffs?

Said handcuffs have just emerged from the box.

JULIET I was trying to make Leo less boring and inept.
Didn't work. I used them to lock my bike mostly.

ALEX So you moved on to Groom Guy.

JULIET He wasn't much cop either but I liked the danger.

ALEX You seem to be still unpacking your stuff Juliet.
Nice basque by the way.

JULIET I know what you're thinking but these are the
kind of things you leave at your boyfriend's flat aren't
they? You don't tend to bring your salad spinner and foot-
spa if you're only staying the odd night.

ALEX I guess. Where did you keep your salad spinner by
the way?

JULIET What?

ALEX Where did you live when you weren't sleeping over
with gentle Leo?

JULIET *is shifty again.*

ALEX Not at the bride's? Please tell me you didn't used to
flat share with the soon-to-be-and-then-suddenly-not-so-
much Mrs Caspar? Did you?

He's right on the money again.

ALEX Oh Juliet.

JULIET *(genuinely puzzled)* How do you not get murdered
more?

ALEX Just lucky I guess. Man, you really do need somewhere to live.

JULIET *(turning on a sixpence)* Anyhow. Now that we've established that you don't need a big bathroom, on account of being a boy and everything…

ALEX We've established no such thing.

JULIET Do you reeeally need the big bedroom? I mean really?

ALEX You're amazing.

JULIET Why do you need such a big flat anyhow? Single man, no friends as a result of Rain-Man-ish personality.

ALEX I need a lot of wall space. For my collections. Why did you want such a big flat: single woman, no friends as a result of unfortunate wedding promiscuity?

JULIET I want kids.

ALEX What?

JULIET Kids. I want lots of kids. Be part of a family. But do it right this time. Thought I'd start here and then move when I'd reached two or three.

ALEX You? Want kids?

> **ALEX** *struggles, knowing his next line is foolhardy.*

ALEX Is that wise? For you to… breed?

JULIET Get lost, I'd be a brilliant Mum.

ALEX Would you?

JULIET Outstanding. I'm a great cook and I'm relaxed about curfews and raves and stuff.

ALEX Yes, you sound ideal material. Who would the father be?

JULIET Not too fussed. I make good money. Leo was strong and pretty, I thought he might do. Groom Guy was a willing donor until his wife cut up rough.

ALEX Very Darwinian. Widening the gene pool.

JULIET Anyway, men aren't important in child rearing after they've made their initial contribution.

This is a bigger sentence than she realises, her damage in a nutshell.

ALEX You've got it all sorted out then.

JULIET Yup.

ALEX Apart from a home for you and all your kids.

JULIET And my basque and my handcuffs.

ALEX You're not getting the big bedroom.

JULIET Okay. The box room is fine for now. Since I'm back to square one on the sperm donors anyhow.

ALEX How did this happen?

JULIET You had a weak moment. A kind moment.

Another subtle sea change has taken place.

ALEX You're a good cook I guess.

JULIET I'm not cooking for you, you sexist misogynistic sexist woman hater.

ALEX Bit harsh. You gave me the nice sandwich.

JULIET Anyway, I'm not cooking for you. Again.

ALEX Well, I wouldn't want you expressing any gratitude for my saving you from a night on the street. Nights on the street in fact.

JULIET And no sex either.

ALEX Sorry?

JULIET You won't be getting any sex. From me. Ever.

ALEX What makes you think I want to have sex with you?

JULIET All men do. Most women too now I think about it. Very inconvenient. It's the hair I think.

ALEX I don't.

JULIET You don't what?

ALEX Want to have sex with you.

JULIET Yes you do.

ALEX No I don't.

JULIET Yes you do. Why else would you suddenly start begging me to move in with you? Into my own flat, ironically.

ALEX I don't want to have sex with you Juliet.

JULIET Are you gay? You weren't very specific about who

you were giving all these wonderful orgasms to. Were they men? Are you queer? Are you gay? Are you a queer-gay-bum-stuffing-arse-bandit, to quote Ben Elton?

ALEX You like Ben Elton?

JULIET You are gay then. Subtle change of subject. You like boys. You're for dudes.

ALEX I don't like boys. I do like Ben Elton. Blackadder at least.

JULIET Blackadder is a work of genius.

ALEX You like Blackadder. I like Blackadder. A breakthrough.

JULIET Everyone likes Blackadder. It's like saying "ooh look, we've both got toes, it must be love".

ALEX It's not like that at all.

JULIET Will you be having men round? I'm not a homophobe but I don't want to hear actual squelching noises.

ALEX I'm not gay, Juliet.

JULIET Maybe you should go in the box room if you are going to be having lots of noisy gay sex. Less of an echo.

ALEX You can't have the big bedroom. No matter how many children you pop out.

JULIET Do you hate kids? A lot of the gays aren't keen apparently.

ALEX I like order. Kids aren't good if you like order.

He's introspective for the first time, knowing this isn't a good way to be.

JULIET Yeah, you're gay as a maypole. You're a big gay neat freak collector poofter.

ALEX It's interesting to me that you think that any man who doesn't want to have sex with you is gay.

JULIET Like I say, all heterosexual men want to get busy with me. That's why I'm a bit… *(struggling for the word)* … prickly. Initially. Necessary defence mechanism.

ALEX You're vile, sorry 'prickly', because otherwise everybody hits on you?

JULIET Something like that.

ALEX Well, no need on my account. I'm not interested in you.

JULIET Really, why not?

ALEX I like my girls to be less… vile. Prickly I mean.

JULIET But I just told you that the prickly-aka-vileness is a… front. That means the moment I drop the front you'll be all over me like a rash and we'll be back to square one.

ALEX You reckon?

JULIET Racing certainty.

ALEX Best not to drop it then. You can be my vile, prickly flat mate. Saves having a guard dog.

There's a long pause.

JULIET So. We're platonic flat mates then?

ALEX Seems that way.

JULIET Fancy.

ALEX Well, since you don't have much to unpack you can help me. Take those boxes with L.R on them into the living room.

JULIET What's that you say?

ALEX Boxes. Living room. You. Take.

> **JULIET** *looks genuinely thrown. Then she shrugs and picks up the smallest box and carries it out. While she's away* **ALEX** *takes out another type case and hangs it.*

> **JULIET** *returns and shows no sign of taking another box. Instead she takes a long glug of cold water from the sink tap and feigns exhaustion.*

JULIET It's hot.

ALEX What?

JULIET Hot in here. Outside too.

ALEX Like I said. It's summer.

JULIET Yes. I suppose.

> *Seeing this is going no further he turns and unpacks more framed collections.* **JULIET** *watches him carefully. He's wearing just a white, tight fitting vest and cargo shorts with bare feet. He's kind of skinny ripped and, while his hair is un-styled, it's hard to deny he is quite attractive himself.*

JULIET It's all right for men.

ALEX Is it?

JULIET You can take your shirts off in public and nobody bats an eyelid. Most men have much bigger breasts than me and yet you can take your shirts off and everything is hunky dory.

ALEX I'm confused. Do you want to take your shirt off?

JULIET See. I told you, the minute I drop my front you'd be asking to see my front.

ALEX I didn't ask. You started talking about wanting to take your top off and I was just trying to establish why.

JULIET It's hot. I'm hot. You're in your vest and I've got a thickish denim shirt on and you've got me moving boxes.

ALEX Box. So far. Just the one.

JULIET If I take off my shirt will you be able to contain your base, caveman urges?

ALEX I reckon. As long as you keep up a strong flow of vile-stroke-prickly comments it should be okay. Are you wearing a bra?

JULIET Why. Would that tip you over the edge? If I weren't?

ALEX No.

JULIET Usually I don't. But today I am.

ALEX Okay then.

JULIET But it's a very pretty Victoria's Secret number. Might as well not be there in many respects.

ALEX I'm relaxed either way. As long as you actually move a few boxes I'm relaxed either way. Shirt on, shirt off. Relaxed.

JULIET You said relaxed three times.

ALEX Did I?

JULIET Kind of establishing the opposite.

ALEX Look. I'm emptying boxes, you're moving them. You could be naked or wearing a gorilla costume for all the attention I'll be paying you.

JULIET Okay then.

She takes off her denim shirt revealing the aforementioned pretty bra and a previously only hinted at... killer body.

ALEX See. Nothing.

JULIET Well, that's a relief. Now I can move these boxes unmolested.

ALEX Go on then.

JULIET Go on then what?

ALEX Move another box.

JULIET This one's quite big.

ALEX Do you want a hand?

JULIET Yes please.

ALEX Rightyho.

JULIET Rightyho?

ALEX I meant 'right'.

JULIET Come on then.

ALEX Right.

> *He steps over to her. They stand either side of the largest box then squat at the same moment and lift it into the air.*

> *They stand face to face over the lifted box. Neither move.*

ALEX To me, or to you?

JULIET What?

ALEX To me, or to you?

JULIET To you. I guess.

> *At the same moment they lean in and kiss each other with equal passion. The kiss is incredibly intense and held for an age. Then, with unspoken mutual agreement and matching timing, they swing the box to one side.*

> *It lands with a crash which reflects the force with which their bodies come together.*

> *Their writhing kiss eventually breaks. They stand breathing irregularly.*

ALEX Blimey.

JULIET That was unexpected.

ALEX Yes.

JULIET Not what you'd expect.

ALEX Given that we've only known each other 40 minutes.

JULIET And have hated each other for 39 of them.

ALEX I didn't like you much in that last minute either.

JULIET Your kiss says otherwise.

ALEX Maybe this isn't such a good idea.

JULIET Maybe not.

ALEX We've only known each other for, well, 41 minutes now.

JULIET That 40th minute was a humdinger though.

ALEX Yes.

JULIET But maybe we shouldn't go any further.

ALEX Into a 42nd minute.

JULIET Of kissing.

ALEX Might be unwise.

JULIET Mind you...

ALEX What?

JULIET Don't think too much harm has been done. So far.

ALEX If we stop now.

JULIET If we go no further.

ALEX Going further might be not so smart.

JULIET We haven't gone too far yet.

ALEX If we stop, you know, now.

JULIET Yes. Generally speaking, I find things don't go really tits up until the sex happens…

There's a long pause while they get their breath completely back.

Then they fall on each other, frantically pulling off their remaining clothes. Curtain falls for the end of the first act.

ACT TWO

Int. The house. Day.

ALEX *stands motionless, dressed in a thick coat, staring at a large, lumpy object (or objects) under a white dust sheet. The flat is just as bare as when we last saw it but there are some signs of gentrification.*

We hear the front door open and **JULIET** *enters, also wearing a winter coat. They are ten years older than when we last saw them fighting to get naked…*

ALEX You're early.

JULIET Things to do. Can't stay long.

Her eyes flick to the window. **ALEX**'s *follow them. He doesn't like what he sees but doesn't comment.*

ALEX How long do you have?

JULIET Half an hour.

ALEX Half an hour isn't enough.

JULIET 45 minutes tops. We have to be somewhere.

The atmosphere, already chilly, chills further.

JULIET It's cold. Put the heating on.

ALEX Is it worth it? Since we'll only be here for half-an-hour-45-minutes tops?

JULIET *(simply)* It's cold. I'm cold.

ALEX Well if you're cold, you're cold.

JULIET Startling insight.

ALEX Thanks. I do what I can.

JULIET If only that were true.

ALEX Well you 'do' enough for two so I guess we balance each other out.

> **JULIET** *makes a half hearted attempt to fiddle with a dial in the fireplace, quickly giving up in frustration.*

JULIET Balanced. Past tense.

ALEX So my lawyers tell me. Would you like me to put the heating on?

JULIET Yes, why don't you?

ALEX Even though it won't warm up until we're about to leave?

JULIET *(deep irony)* Can't imagine why we're getting divorced.

> *He too reaches into the fireplace where the thermo is clearly somewhat inconveniently located.*

ALEX I'm putting it on 15.

> *There is a distant whoosh of a boiler firing up somewhere in the house. While his back is turned* **JULIET** *sneaks a peek under the dust sheet but whatever is under there seems of no interest whatsoever.*

ALEX That's a compromise temperature. You want it
on, I don't think it's worth it... as we'll be long gone
before it warms up... Therefore 15: the temperature of
compromise.

JULIET If you put it on 15 it's not worth putting it on at
all. Put it on 30 so it warms up faster.

ALEX That's not the way a thermostat works. The
thermo just tells the boiler when to stop boiling. When
its reached the required temperature. It doesn't affect
the speed with which it heats up. Putting it on 30 won't
fire up the secret backup super-boiler we installed for
when we want the house to heat up instantly. Because we
haven't installed one.

JULIET Some men are kind. Some men just beat their
wives with heavy objects...

ALEX Put it on 30 and you just make the house really hot
about an hour after we've left.

JULIET ... Others merely steal all their money and run
off with the nanny...

ALEX Just trying to explain how heating systems actually
work. You could see it as educational.

JULIET ... Still further men just tie their partners to the
bed and set the house on fire...

ALEX One way to warm up.

JULIET ... But not you. You go for mental torture. That's
what those bloody McDonald's toys are aren't they?
Mental torture in all the colours of the rainbow.

ALEX I'll put it on 30 if it makes you happy.

JULIET Why water-board suspects when you can simply show them your complete set of autographs from every man who's walked on the moon? Framed in order of touchdown.

ALEX I like to collect things. I'm a collector.

JULIET That's an epic understatement. Like Hitler saying 'I'm not too keen on the smell of bagels'.

> **ALEX** *opens a bill that he collected from the doorstep on the way in.*

ALEX *(habitually educating)* Did you know that every man who walked on the moon was a first born son? All 12 of them.

JULIET Yes! I know that because you bloody told me! Many, many times.

ALEX Interesting though huh? Sibling order. Lasting effect of.

JULIET *(loaded)* Since when were you interested in sibling anything?

ALEX Just an observation.

> *The conversation has turned a tricky corner.* **ALEX** *flicks his eyes back to the bill but doesn't read it.*

JULIET If we get on with this we could be done in 30 minutes. I've got a thing.

ALEX Oh, it's really not worth putting the heating on then. I'll switch it off again.

JULIET Touch that dial and I'll beat you to death with your collection of Replica light-sabers.

ALEX That could take a while. They aren't hugely sturdy.

JULIET I'm persistent.

ALEX Besides, I've already packed them.

JULIET Oh.

ALEX I packed all my stuff yesterday.

JULIET Oh. Did you? All your collections?

He opens a door off the kitchen and they look out.

JULIET So you did.

ALEX Then I packed your stuff.

JULIET Really?

ALEX What was left of it. Living room.

He gestures vaguely to the doorway. She goes to check.

ALEX My stuff in our room. Your stuff in box room.

JULIET Oh.

ALEX Less of your stuff, obviously. So it was no trouble.

JULIET Oh. Why are we here then? You said we had to pack.

ALEX The joint stuff.

JULIET Joint stuff?

ALEX The stuff that's not mine or yours. The stuff that's… ours.

JULIET Oh.

ALEX You're saying 'oh' a lot. Did you know?

JULIET Oh. Well. It's just... this is not what I thought we'd be...

ALEX *(at the door)* I tried to... simplify the process. That's mine, this is yours and then there's the stuff that's er... neither. We need to go through it and see where it goes to live now. Now it can't live with... us.

JULIET I would have come back and helped. If I'd known.

ALEX You put most of the furniture on eBay. That helped.

JULIET I thought there'd be bubble wrapping to be done.

ALEX There was. But I did it.

JULIET I like to pop the bubbles.

ALEX I know...

He hands her a little piece of bubble wrap. **JULIET** *gives it a couple of exploratory pops.*

JULIET Not as much fun as I remember.

ALEX Know the feeling.

JULIET Is there much?

ALEX Much what?

JULIET Much joint stuff.

ALEX Less than you'd think. Come see.

He removes the dust sheet under which an eclectic pile of objects are neatly arranged.

JULIET Gosh. Quite an eclectic collection. Even you'd have trouble finding a thematic link for that lot.

ALEX They are all things we bought together. In the last ten years.

JULIET Apart from that.

ALEX All things that we both… liked.

He means loved. A moment's pause as they take in the objects.

JULIET The pile says we don't have much in common. Irreconcilable differences made flesh. *(mumbled)* Well, made metal and wood and plastic.

ALEX Oh, I don't know.

JULIET *(flat)* A locked sea chest, an old tandem, a french bed, a stuffed puppy, a print, a bowl full of pebbles, some candle sticks and a tin chicken that lays little tin eggs. Or would do if we hadn't lost them all over the years.

ALEX Ha! That's where you're wrong!

ALEX picks up a small tin chicken with a flourish, winds it and sets it walking towards JULIET. After an age it gives a metallic squawk and plops out a tiny tin egg.

JULIET *(unmoved)* You found an egg.

Another squawk, another plop.

ALEX Two actually. One under the coal scuttle and one in my tool box. I thought I'd found a third down the back of the dentist's chair... but it turned out to be an ancient macadamia nut.

JULIET *(unmoved)* The eBay guy came for the dentist's chair?

ALEX Yes. He couldn't believe his luck. A '57 Steinbecker, four motors still working, some damage to lower leather. Collectors' item.

JULIET But he came?

ALEX Yes.

JULIET And he gave you money?

ALEX Yes.

JULIET And he took it away?

ALEX Yes.

JULIET Finally.

ALEX But...

JULIET But?

ALEX But it got stuck in the door so...

JULIET So?

ALEX I bought it back off him.

An angry silence. On **JULIET**'s *side at least.*

ALEX My new place has a little bay window where a dentist chair will sit really well.

JULIET How will you get it out?

ALEX What?

JULIET If you and the eBay guy couldn't get it out how will you and no eBay guy get it out?

ALEX Oh. Well. It goes out through the window okay. If you take the sash out.

JULIET Something you neglected to tell the eBay guy.

ALEX There was something not quite right about him.

JULIET There was something not quite right about HIM??

> **ALEX** *feels things are slipping away. He fiddles nervously with something in his pocket. The thing wires suddenly causing him to stop fiddling with it and withdraw his hand.*

ALEX Shall we talk about this stuff?

JULIET *(ice cold)* Okay well, I don't want any of these things so they're all yours if you do.

ALEX What? *(sad)* You don't want anything?

JULIET Not really.

ALEX I thought I'd have to fight you for the chicken.

JULIET You were wrong. I'm through fighting.

ALEX Why did the chicken commit suicide?

JULIET I don't know.

ALEX To get to the other side.

JULIET That's funny.

ALEX You say 'that's funny' instead of laughing.

JULIET It wasn't laugh out loud funny.

ALEX You don't even want the tandem?

JULIET What would I want with a tandem now?

ALEX You and Hector could go riding.

JULIET Hugo.

ALEX Whatever.

JULIET You know his name of course. You know the name of the, the, *(reaching for the most obscure thing she can conjure up)* the guy who filled the Saturn Five rockets up with petrol. You probably know his middle name. You never forget anything.

ALEX Werner Von Braun. No middle name in fact. Unless you count Von. And it was liquid hydrogen. Not petrol.

JULIET I rest my case.

ALEX Veteran of the German v2 programme. Spirited away from the Russians by the Americans just before the war ended. Rather unpleasant Nazi actually. Don't know why I bothered hunting down his autograph.

JULIET So you know Hugo's name perfectly well.

ALEX Cliff-walking by Hugo first.

JULIET What?

ALEX If you want to remember someone's name you have

to put it in a memorable and relevant sentence. Cliff walking by Hugo first. Old joke. In which Hugo gets to walk off a cliff. Perfect.

JULIET So why did you call him Hector?

ALEX To... ahm... annoy you.

JULIET Congratulations. It was a runaway success.

ALEX Not big on cycling then, Hugo-stroke-Hector?

JULIET He has an Aston Martin.

ALEX's turn to be frosty.

ALEX Okay. I'll keep the tandem.

There's a tiny, almost imperceptible change in **JULIET**, *as though she knows she's gone too far now.*

JULIET You can still use it as a bike. Even without someone on the back I mean. *(pause)* And you can give people lifts back from parties.

ALEX You can go now.

JULIET What?

ALEX is back to fiddling with the thing in his pocket.

ALEX You can go now. Since you don't want any of the stuff. There's no point in your being here. The things you left behind are all packed. The movers are coming tomorrow morning. There's nothing else that needs...

JULIET I think I do want the chicken actually. Now it's got eggs.

ALEX Too late. You said you didn't want anything. That's legally binding.

JULIET No it's not.

ALEX Morally binding then.

JULIET You offered me the tandem after I'd said I didn't want anything. It didn't seem morally binding then. When you were offering me the tandem.

ALEX Well we had some good times on the tandem. I thought you might like it. Despite surrendering your moral rights in a rash fit of pique.

JULIET You seemed keen to go through things one by one until I mentioned Hugo's car.

ALEX I don't care about Hugo's Aston Martin. At least not as much as you do, clearly.

JULIET I want the chicken.

ALEX Yes it's all about accumulating wealth with you isn't it Juliet?

JULIET We paid £3.50 for it.

ALEX Five euros. You can't even remember the country.

JULIET I factored the exchange rate into my calculations.

ALEX You didn't. You're just a good improvisor.

JULIET How could I forget our first weekend away? I'm not that unromantic.

ALEX You're exactly that unromantic. We went to Whitstable on our first weekend away. Paris was second.

JULIET I meant our first weekend away-away. Abroad away.

ALEX You're a busker. An unromantic busker.

JULIET I want the chicken. If you're having the tandem I should get the chicken.

ALEX I didn't particularly want the tandem. I got it by default. Because you didn't. Too busy squirming around on the leather seats of Huuugo's Aston bloody Martin.

JULIET I want it. I thought you wanted me to want some of this junk? You think I'm a hard hearted bitch for not wanting any of this stuff. So. I'll have the chicken.

Another pause, another subtle change in the undercurrent.

ALEX You can have the chicken.

JULIET Thanks.

ALEX If you can remember anything about when and where we bought it.

JULIET Persil.

ALEX What?

JULIET We were there because of Persil.

ALEX You're speaking in tongues now Juliet.

JULIET It was a special offer. If you bought ridiculously large quantities of Persil and kept the pack tops eventually you got two free train tickets to Paris. We were young and poorer than church mice's poverty stricken cousins but… We worked out that if we slept on the train

and stayed up all Saturday night we wouldn't need a
hotel. The whole weekend would be free apart from food.
So we went to Paris and bought a tin chicken. *(having
slightly impressed herself)* … From an Algerian man with not
many teeth who sold tin chickens on the pavement. Made
them himself. Later we made love under a bridge by the
Seine at five in the morning with the sun just coming
up over the Eiffel Tower. You made me come so hard I
thought the top of my head would flip clean off.

Another beat. Another shift.

ALEX Okay.

JULIET Okay what?

ALEX You can have the chicken. Because you remember
quite well.

JULIET Thanks.

ALEX I'm keeping the eggs though. I worked hard to find
them and it was in fact OMO.

JULIET OMO! Bugger!

ALEX Close but no cigar on the washing powder offer
front.

JULIET You can't have an egg laying chicken without
eggs.

ALEX You could use macadamia nuts. They look pretty
similar to the uninitiated.

JULIET What will you do with your two tin eggs?

ALEX Put them on the back seat of my tandem.
For company.

JULIET You're just being petty now. OMO, Persil, what's the difference?

ALEX Persil turned out to be more commercially viable in the long run.

JULIET Keep the damn eggs. You can start a collection of tiny tin food. You'll be happy as a pig in shit.

ALEX Do you want to go through the rest of the stuff? Or are you happy with your chicken?

JULIET No. Now you've stolen my eggs I'll fight you for the rest of the stuff.

ALEX Excellent. Do you want tea while we're working our way through? I left out two bags and some liberated UHT milk pots.

JULIET Sounds delicious.

> **ALEX** *fills the kettle. Then the front door bell rings.*
> **ALEX**'*s hand again goes to his pocket to be soothed by the unseen little object secreted there.*

JULIET Who's that?

ALEX Ahm... movers.

JULIET You said they were coming tomorrow.

ALEX They are.

JULIET And they've come 24 hours early in case the traffic's bad?

ALEX Some movers are coming tomorrow and some, ahm, today.

JULIET 'Ahm'

ALEX 'Ahm?'

JULIET When you are feeling shifty you say 'Ahm'.

The bell rings again.

JULIET Better answer that. Don't want him going away and leaving you with just the one mover.

ALEX Her actually.

JULIET Her?

He exits and we hear the door open.

AMANDA *(distant)* Hi Alex. I'm so, so sorry, I'm late! Unbelievable traffic. Traffic that's really very hard to believe even for the especially traffically gullible. Which is me, incidentally.

Suspiciously friendly and garrulous this mover. **ALEX** *tries to be more formal.*

ALEX It isn't a problem. Ahm. Not much of a problem anyhow… come in.

AMANDA I'm just so, you know, excited. Big day for me. *(cheery correction)* For us!

ALEX *enters with a young woman at his side. She is blonde, slim, pretty and expensively dressed.*

ALEX Sorry about the cold…

A comment not lost on **JULIET**.

ALEX … Amanda this is Juliet, my wife. For now.

JULIET Hi. Ex-wife. To be. Wife-for-now-ex-wife-to-be. Quite a mouthful but important to be precise.

AMANDA I guess.

JULIET *(as if addressing a class of six year olds)* What are you excited about? Precisely.

AMANDA Oh. Ahm. The boxes. I guess. Contents thereof.

JULIET 'Ahm'. Catchy that 'ahm'. All the rage.

ALEX We're still dividing up some stuff in here. Do you mind helping yourself? Shout if any of the boxes are too heavy.

AMANDA Oh. Right thanks. I've brought the...

ALEX *(cutting her off)* We'll do all that later.

AMANDA Okay.

ALEX They're all just in there, labelled and everything.

AMANDA Great.

She seems like she wants to stay. But leaves.

JULIET She seems nice. Your 'mover'.

ALEX Yes.

JULIET Pretty.

ALEX Is she?

JULIET I'd say so. Very pretty. Slim too. Almost skinny. And well dressed.

ALEX I didn't notice.

JULIET Pretty. Skinny. Expensively attired. *(casual)* Your typical moving man in fact.

ALEX She's just out of the phone book. Local. Do you want Ripjaws?

> **ALEX** *holds up the stuffed puppy. A rather misshapen sausage dog. This is another temperature changer.*

JULIET No. I don't think so.

ALEX I couldn't throw him away. Poor Ripjaws.

JULIET Ridiculous name for a sausage dog.

ALEX That was the point.

JULIET No it wasn't. The point was to bring some mess into your life, our lives. To get you ready for, to help you see that… order isn't everything. That mess can be…

> *She runs out of sentence, too hard to complete. Pause.*

ALEX It was certainly a mess after you backed the car over him.

JULIET That was unfortunate, poor Ripjaws. As you say. *(to the very dead dog)* Sorry. Again. For everything.

ALEX *(ventriloquist voice)* No groblem. Anyone can gake a gistake.

JULIET He proved a point anyway. About us.

ALEX *(still ventriloquist)* What goint?

JULIET Unwilling father, incompetent mother. If you

have both you're basically... stuffed.

ALEX You weren't incompetent.

JULIET I drove over him. Then, when I went back to see what the bump was, I drove over him some more. He's better off staying with you.

ALEX Okay.

JULIET Take him off the stand and he'd make a fine draft excluder. Maybe he'll will come in handy for you and the moving manlady.

ALEX Juliet, there's no rea–

JULIET Just keep the damn dog!! I don't want the dog. I never wanted this dog or any dog. I wanted a baby.

ALEX We tal–

JULIET I know we talked about it! I know we agreed before we got married that we didn't, that we shouldn't, that we couldn't... What with my unsociable work hours and your unsociable collections. We agreed. I know. But I changed my mind. I wanted, I needed and you, and you, and you... didn't.

> *The first ugly pause.* **ALEX** *clicks the kettle back on. While he waits for it to boil he takes the object from his pocket. It's the little McDonald's dinosaur.*

ALEX Do you want that tea?

JULIET Yes why not. Tea cures everything, doesn't it? Who needs kids when you can have tea?

> **JULIET** *sees the dinosaur but does not remember it. Another small heartbreak for* **ALEX***. He puts it back in*

his pocket.

ALEX Shall we just divide up the rest of the stuff and not have this fight again?

JULIET No. Let's forget about dividing up this pointless heap of junk and have this fight one more time for fun shall we? Let's have it out one more time for the sheer bloody laughs.

ALEX Okay. Let's. Tell me *(parroting)* 'one more time' how my interest in collecting things justifies your infidelity?

JULIET Ha! That's not the fight! That's not the main course! That's the sodding sorbet. No, actually, it's the bleeding pointless After Eight that comes with the bill.

ALEX Not to me.

JULIET No, not to you. You didn't even notice the previous ten years where I worked my tits off in a red hot stinking kitchen... 'You must follow your dream Jools, money doesn't matter'... All so you could stay home hunting down the-the-the Portuguese variation of the Sergeant Pepper cover. Or the only Pepsi can ever to have two ring pulls. Or the-or the-or the Christ knows what plastic Star Wars figure that's never been taken out of the box because no child alive could ever be arsed to play with it on the grounds of its total obscurity! (suddenly exhausted) Mother Teresa would have gone out and shagged Hugo if she'd lived in this flat slaving away paying for everything until her *(drying up herself)* womb dried up...

There's a knock at the door. **AMANDA** *enters.*

ALEX Oh, hi.

AMANDA Sorry to disturb you Alex but... there's a couple that are, ahm, a little heavy. I wonder if…

ALEX Sure. Help yourself to tea, it's fresh into the pot.

AMANDA Oh. No. I…

But he's gone, leaving the two women alone together.
***AMANDA** seems wide eyed. Perhaps with curiosity. Who*
is this shouty woman with the sweet ex?

JULIET Do you take sugar?

AMANDA Oh. No. No thanks.

JULIET Of course not. Milk?

AMANDA Yes please.

JULIET Careful.

AMANDA Of what?

JULIET The tea. It's hot.

*She means 'watch your step punk' but **AMANDA** doesn't*
clock.

AMANDA Oh thanks. *(pause)* Hey, beautiful chest.

She's seen the old sea chest.

JULIET *(Groucho)* Why thanks honey, but you're not
my thing.

AMANDA I meant the sea chest.

JULIET *(eye roll)* I know.

AMANDA Amazing ornate lock.

JULIET Oh it's not ornate. It's bloody impregnable. We bought it in a junk shop and never been able to open it. Could be full of diamonds and rubies.

AMANDA Could be.

JULIET Or a body perhaps. Captured and killed by forgetful pirates.

AMANDA A chest full of romance.

JULIET Or old newspapers and surgical supports.

AMANDA Still. Fun not knowing.

JULIET That was always Alex's theory. Or maybe just his excuse for not getting out his tool kit and having a proper go. Do you want it?

AMANDA Don't you?

JULIET Not really.

AMANDA It must be so difficult for you both.

JULIET Difficult?

AMANDA Dividing up all these fascinating things.

JULIET We're just pretending to fight over all this crap. A fond goodbye for the dysfunctional.

    AMANDA *eyes the chest again.*

AMANDA I'm sure Alex will want it.

JULIET Are you now? *(sizing her up again)* Must be a slight drawback…

AMANDA Drawback?

JULIET Not being able to pick stuff up. In your game.

AMANDA My game?

JULIET Removals.

AMANDA Oh I see, ha, no I'm not really, ahm, a removals person.

JULIET Noooo, really? What is your line of work then?

    AMANDA *is more steely than her girlish voice indicates.*

AMANDA Alex asked me to be discreet. Maybe it's best if you two... talked it over. Thanks for the tea.

JULIET You're welcome... *(quietly after she's gone)* ... don't let the door bang on your smug, boney arse on the way out.

ALEX *(outside the kitchen)* I put the two big ones in. Sorry, I should have thought.

    ALEX *speaks warmly to her. Not as to a stranger.*

AMANDA *(also off)* No problem. I'll just finish my tea, put the rest in and, ahm, get out of your hair.

    ALEX *returns.*

JULIET Nice girl.

ALEX Nice enough.

JULIET Sure you should be letting her carry all those boxes. Wouldn't want her to snap in two before you've even moved in together.

ALEX I'm not moving in with her. You're mistaking me for you.

JULIET You could do worse.

ALEX Is that what you think?

JULIET Well, yes, she's a pretty little foetus and has a bit of spunk to her...

ALEX No. I mean is that what you think? Do you think I stopped you having children so I could live off the money you made? Is that really what you believe?

JULIET Blimey Alex. That sounds surprisingly like an adult conversation. Sure you wouldn't rather talk about divvying up the last few objects?

ALEX I was always happy to talk.

JULIET Yes but you weren't often happy to turn around Al. To put down your magnifying glass and tweezers and actually talk. To me.

ALEX You were harder to talk to when you were in someone else's bed.

JULIET *(turning on a sixpence)* I'll take the bed actually.

ALEX What?

JULIET The bed.

> *She knocks the bedstead with her knuckles and examines a little old tag on its wall side.*

JULIET I'll take it. That'll make it two all. You have the tandem and ripjaws. I'll have the tin chicken and the french bed.

ALEX Okay.

JULIET Lots of good memories in this bed. You might
be agoraphobic, anti-social and perhaps a teeny bit
autistic but you've always known how to make a girl's
bells ringadingding.

ALEX Thanks.

JULIET I guess you collected sex tricks as well. Maybe
you're collecting some more from mover-girl?

ALEX Ironic that you are the jealous one, huh?

JULIET I could have used a bit more jealousy over the
years actually. If you lost a copy of the Fantastic Four,
original Stan Lee, Edition Number 17, some pages slightly
damaged, you'd be frantic. But if I came home late on a
Friday night it would be "Hi babe, did you remember to
pick up my balsa wood and glue?"

ALEX Not sure you're in a position to say I didn't care
about you. That's not my boyfriend waiting outside in the
Aston Martin.

She's slightly flustered, busted.

JULIET I have to get going soon.

ALEX So you keep saying.

Ugly pause.

JULIET I'm not saying I'm covered in glory and standing
on the toppiest peak of the moral high ground. I'm just
saying you love only plastic and vinyl and cardboard and
photographic paper. You're like that stupid chest:
firmly closed.

ALEX I love you. Loved you.

JULIET Oh yeah? Where's your 'me' collection then?
Where's your Juliet Stone scrapbook? *(suddenly clinical)* You
say I'm unromantic. What about you? You've got laminated
Beatles, Oasis, Blur and Dexy's Midnight freaking
Runners gig tickets… Have you got a single memento of
anything WE have done together? There's enough framed,
alphabetised, mounted, freeze dried, meaningless crap in
this house to fill four museums 'that-nobody-would-bother-
going-to, incidentally' but do you have a single birthday
card I sent you?? A picture of me where I'm not wearing a
wedding dress and a slightly doubtful expression?
Do you??

There's a long pause.

JULIET No answer? No need to answer.

ALEX Would you like the big glass bowl with the pebbles
in it?

JULIET Subtle change of subject there, cupcake.

ALEX I wasn't changing the subject.

JULIET Why would I want a poxy glass bowl full of even
poxier pebbles.

ALEX How else will you keep score?

JULIET *(suddenly less confident)* What are you talking about?

ALEX It's time to pour them out and start again isn't it?
Though, of course, you started the process a while ago.

JULIET Don't know what you're talking about. I'll take
the bowl if you want me to take the bowl. It's just a stupid
bowl.

ALEX No. It's not.

JULIET It's not?

ALEX It's a special bowl. It means a lot to you. And it meant a lot to me when I found out what it was.

JULIET A bowl. With pebbles in.

ALEX That fills up and then empties.

JULIET If I found a nice stone I used to like to pick it up and, ahm, put it in a bowl.

ALEX For the first year of our relationship you put a pebble in the bowl every time we made love. Then after the first year you took a pebble out every time we made love. The theory being the bowl never empties.

JULIET Bugger. You worked that out?

ALEX Of course not. I read the same article in Cosmo as you did.

JULIET *(mental note)* Never leave your old mags in a pile by the toilet.

ALEX A man must sit and read.

JULIET I wanted to prove it was a stupid theory. I wanted to prove that things would stay as frantic and hungry and sweaty and dirty as they were at the beginning. I wanted the bowl to fill up fast and empty fast. I wanted the stupid bowl to get empty.

ALEX Nobody's bowl empties Juliet. What are you fourteen?

JULIET I think that's sad.

ALEX It's not. After you're done showing off you start… going to… movies going for walks and yes, eventually, inevitably, going to sleep. It doesn't mean anything other than… sex isn't everything. It certainly doesn't mean the sex is bad.

JULIET I never said it did.

ALEX But still you wanted the pebbles to empty out?

JULIET Yes! I wanted pebble evacuation! I'm the absolute embodiment of all evil aren't I? Because I wanted you to make love to me more! Because I wanted you to express love for something that you didn't buy in Camden Passage! Because I wanted a tangible sign that you, that you, that you actually… loved me… sometimes… you bloody locked-in syndrome victim!

> *She gulps one of those involuntary lungfuls of air that count as tears for people who can't cry anymore.* **ALEX** *has a thousand answers but none that make it into actual speech.*

JULIET *(calmer, suddenly spent)* Why didn't you sneak pebbles out? If you knew, why didn't you help? Legally or illegally? Why didn't you stick it in more or take them out more?

Another subtle change.

ALEX Because that's cheating. And cheating is bad.

JULIET *(another sixpence moment)* Hugo likes to do it all the time.

ALEX Whoopee.

JULIET *(slightly punctured)* He just doesn't know how to do it. Practice it seems, does not always make perfect.

ALEX But think of his excellent credit profile.

JULIET Sod off. And you can keep the bowl. Let it be a lesson to you.

ALEX What's the lesson?

JULIET How should I know? Anyway, I'm having the bed so you get the bowl.

ALEX You can have the bed if you can remember where we bought it and how much it cost.

JULIET Brighton. Boot sale. 60 quid.

ALEX Blimey.

JULIET Ha!

ALEX You never remember stuff. Romantic stuff at least.

JULIET Dope.

ALEX Why am I a dope?

JULIET Because if you want to win a memory game you ought to check if there's still a Brighton Market sticker on the back of the headboard with the price written on it.

ALEX Oh. Rats.

He checks and finds the label. A mobile rings.

JULIET *(answering)* Hi... no... no, it's taking longer than I... tell them to wait, you're the boss aren't you? ... I'll be ten minutes, turn on the engine if you're cold... no, not in the slightest... *(he's saying I love you)* ... That's nice... *(he's asking her why she isn't saying it back)* ... Because I'm standing opposite my soon-to-be-ex husband, fool... okay. Bye.

There's the distant sound of an expensive engine firing up. **ALEX** *watches through the kitchen window.*

ALEX Got his very own hole in the ozone, has he?

JULIET Sunbathing in December, a workable UK wine industry, personally I struggle to see the downside of global warming.

ALEX I suppose climate change might wipe out the bastard squirrels.

JULIET Oh not still with the squirrels.

ALEX Herds of squirrel-eating tigers sweeping across Hampstead Heath…

JULIET Tigers don't herd. They kill herds.

ALEX Yes! Herds of squirrels! That'd be worth losing a couple of Pacific atolls for.

JULIET You are the only human being alive who hates squirrels.

ALEX Did you hear the latest?

JULIET Squirrels found to be behind 9/11?

ALEX Worse.

JULIET The squirrels have done something worse than murdering 3,000 innocent people?

ALEX Okay. Not worse. But nearly as bad.

JULIET You are a ridiculous human being.

ALEX They nested in my Corgi toys!

JULIET Maybe I was a bit generous with the 'human being' classification.

ALEX Well, not in the actual toys. But the scheming bastards broke into the loft, tore the boxes into pieces and made the pieces into nests so they could make more bastard squirrel-bastards!!

JULIET *(knowing this will wind him up)* Gosh! Aren't they clever?

ALEX Clever?? Clever!! They were mint in the box! Not a finger print, not a spec of dust. Virgin Corgi! The Avengers! Steed still on his little stand by the green Bentley. Thunderbirds! Lady Penelope in her futuristic pink Roller! It's a desecration by a bunch of RATS IN TAIL MUFFS!!!

JULIET I like it when they sit on their little haunches with their yummy fluffy tails curled up their back and munch on an acorn. Adorable.

ALEX They're vermin! Super vermin! I reckon even the tail thing is a conspiracy. Shave a squirrel and bingo, you've got yourself a rat. I think a bunch of especially smart ones, their intellects sharpened in all those mazes, escaped from a government lab somewhere and got themselves some glue and a box of furry grey pencil cases. Then they were away. Disgusting worm tail into the glue, a quick roll in some pencil case trimmings and suddenly the world is saying LOOK AT THE CUTE SQUIRREL SITTING ON ITS LITTLE HAUNCHES MUNCHING ON MY CORGI TOY BOXES!!!!

JULIET *(pressing an imaginary intercom button)* Sedative for Mr. Arnold.

ALEX They destroyed the value of my Dinky Bond cars through the ages...

JULIET What?

ALEX *(suddenly wanting to change the subject)* Nothing.

> *There's a pause whilst this normally calm, passive*
> *man recovers his composure.* **JULIET** *joins him at the*
> *window.*

JULIET The stick insect looks like she's almost done too.
Shall we divide up what's left and clear out of each other's
lives? Ooh look, she's sitting on the loading deck of her
suspiciously spotless van and giving you a cheery wave.
That's something you don't get from Pickfords.

ALEX *(shouting through the window)* Sorry! Five more
minutes? Thanks!

JULIET *(squinting)* Is that an armoured van?

ALEX Don't be ridiculous. It's just... chunky. What's left?

JULIET What's left? A locked and therefore useless sea
chest, all yours obviously, entwined wedding present
candle sticks, one each? And the Damian Hirst print...
you'd better have that.

ALEX Why do you always rush important stuff?

JULIET No idea. But I'm rushing this unimportant stuff
because your not so secret girlfriend seems to be almost
as impatient as my ozone perforating Hedge Fund
manager.

ALEX They can wait. Don't you want the candle sticks?

JULIET Not especially, should I?

ALEX They were a present from your Dad.

JULIET Well, you can definitely have them then. The creepy old bastard always liked you better than me. Even when I was little and he wasn't due to meet you for 15 years.

ALEX You should call him.

JULIET What, to tell him he's a creepy old bastard? I think he knows.

ALEX You should call him because one day you aren't going to be able to call him. One day soon maybe.

JULIET I don't want to speak to him while he's alive so I very much doubt I'll suddenly want to chatter his ears off once he's dead.

ALEX Lots of people get divorced Jools. Most kids forgive their parents when they stop being kids themselves. And… find out it's not all fun and games, being married.

JULIET He left me when I was four. I left him when he was forty. It's neat numerically speaking and I'd hate to mess that up now.

ALEX You should keep his candle sticks. They are rather beautiful. The way they wrap around each other. A thoughtful wedding gift when you think about it.

JULIET Yes, I'm sure his PA put a lot of thought into it.

ALEX Let's have one each then.

JULIET That's dopey, they are meant to entwine. Won't they fall over without each other? Or at least die of symbolism?

ALEX Maybe. Let's see… nope, they can stand on their own. Just about.

JULIET They don't look right though, do they. Like
Lembit Opik's face.

ALEX A bit lopsided.

JULIET If I keep the bloody candles will you stop telling
me to phone my pigdogslutdad?

ALEX Yes.

JULIET Okay, that means you get the Damien Hirst.
Which is only fair because you're the one who had the
foresight to buy it before the whole shark pickling thing
really took off.

ALEX That's true but you paid half so...

JULIET You should have it. I want you to have it. Might come
in handy.

ALEX *(bristling)* Why?

JULIET Why what?

ALEX Why might it 'come in handy'?

JULIET You drive me insane, you know that?

ALEX I do know that. But why particularly on this point?

JULIET Because I'M DOING WHAT YOU WANT. I'm
trying to do what you want. I'm going through all this stuff
pretending it matters because it's what you asked me to do.
Because you want these things, these pointless inanimate
objects, to mean something. So you don't feel like the
last ten years were a complete waste of time. And then,
when I do my best to join in, you start questioning why
I'm joining in! Nelson Mandela would set up a 'Lies and
Recrimination Committee' if he lived with you.

ALEX Why would a print be 'handy'?

JULIET You know why.

ALEX I don't.

JULIET You do. You're just pretending you don't.

ALEX Humour me.

JULIET Because it's worth some money isn't it? Aren't you broke?

> *A horrible pause. Another subtle sea change.* **JULIET** *tries to make it less nakedly humiliating.*

JULIET I feel bad enough about the whole 'Getting-caught-having-sex-and-thinking-oh-well-lets-get-divorced-'cos-we-ain't-happy-anyhow' extravaganza without you dying of scurvy to boot. So you keep it.

ALEX 'I'm' not 'we'.

JULIET You're not wee?

ALEX You said 'we' weren't that happy. But I was, so it's just you. 'I' in the original sentence.

JULIET Really? You didn't laugh much for a happy person.

ALEX I was like you with the suicidal chicken joke. I was happy. Just not laugh out loud happy.

JULIET Well I need laugh out loud happy. Sometimes.

ALEX That's because you're an extrovert and I'm an introvert.

JULIET You said it.

ALEX Introverts need space, extroverts need people. I looked it up.

JULIET Okay, well, I went out and got myself a person, leaving you more space. So we're all square, right?

But her words sound tougher than she does.

ALEX *(defeated)* Take the print. In case Hugo Hedge-Fund turns out to be exactly the kind of toss-pot cliché demands. And you need… an escape fund.

JULIET What about you? And the scurvy?

ALEX Limes are cheaper than you think. Sure you don't want the sea chest?

JULIET I was desperate for an old trunk that doesn't even open but… turns out Hugo has a wardrobe. Several actually.

ALEX Will you give up work?

JULIET No. The 1950s ended a while ago apparently.

ALEX Will you look after yourself?

JULIET Will you?

ALEX I tried to.

JULIET No, goof, I meant will you look after yourself?

ALEX I know what you meant.

*A big pause. Many things that could and probably should be said. **JULIET** looks out the window.*

JULIET Twiglet is on her way over. Carrying a briefcase full of sex toys by the looks of it, you lucky boy.

ALEX Okay, ahm, crap.

JULIET Don't worry. I'll go out and throw Hugo a raw steak, keep him occupied for another few minutes. Leave you love birds in peace.

> **JULIET** *leaves, passing the returning* **AMANDA** *in the doorway without acknowledging her.*

AMANDA Oh. *(shrug)* Ahm, Alex, I'm really sorry, I've got an auction to get to. Do you mind if we...

ALEX Sure. *(speaking slightly in code in case* **JULIET** *is still in hearing distance)* It doesn't matter about... you don't have to... let's just...

> *Trying to help him end the sentence,* **AMANDA** *hands him some forms.*

AMANDA If you could just sign here. And here. And initial there and there. And there. That's great. And... here we go.

> *She hands him a briefcase which he does not open.*

ALEX Thanks.

AMANDA Aren't you going to count it?

ALEX No. You have an honest face.

AMANDA And you're... sure?

ALEX Pretty sure. You look like Pixar drew you.

AMANDA No, I mean are you sure you really want to sell

all those beautiful things? All your amazing collections.
So complete. So precise. There must be a lot of you in
those trays.

ALEX *(grinning)* Split a bottle of wine and share an
evening's cataloguing with a girl and she thinks she
knows you.

> *We get a glimpse of why* **ALEX** *was successful with girls
> before* **JULIET**. *But just a glimpse.*

AMANDA Did… she make you…

ALEX No.

> **AMANDA** *looks like she might say more. In fact she looks
> like she wants to write her phone number backwards
> on his forehead in indelible ink. But, in the end, she
> doesn't.*

AMANDA Well look, Alex. It was amazing to meet you, can't
believe my luck actually. If there's ever anything else you
want to…

ALEX There won't be.

AMANDA Okay. Well. Good luck.

> *A moment.* **JULIET** *returns.*

ALEX I'll see you out.

AMANDA *(to* **JULIET***)* Bye.

JULIET *(again, as if addressing year three kids)* Byeee.

> *They go into the hall but stay within earshot.* **JULIET**
> *keeps a sly eye on them.*

AMANDA *(off)* Oh, listen. When I moved the last of the boxes I found this. Figured it wasn't part of the...

ALEX *(off)* Oh. No, thanks. That's mine.

AMANDA *(off)* It's beautiful. You have so many beautiful and unusual things.

ALEX *(off)* Had.

AMANDA *(off)* Yeah. Right. Hey, you should try putting it in that old...

ALEX *(off)* Thanks Amanda. Good luck to you too.

> **ALEX** *comes back to the kitchen carrying a brief case and a large, ancient key. He sets them both carefully on the work top casually concealing the key.*

JULIET Blimey. That was either a really elaborate hoax or she really isn't your new popsie.

ALEX I told you. She's a mover.

JULIET With a brand new van, Jimmy Choo's and muscles like knots in spaghetti.

ALEX There wasn't that much.

JULIET A van full. What's with the case?

ALEX Nothing. Forms.

JULIET What about the giant rusty key?

ALEX You were spying on us?

JULIET Little bit. I was hoping you'd grab her miniscule boobies in the goodbye clinch so I could feel a bit better about everything.

ALEX Sorry I couldn't be more helpful.

JULIET So.

ALEX So?

JULIET What's with the case? And the key? And where's all your stuff going if it's not going to her place?

He looks at her for the longest time. Then...

ALEX *(utterly drained and defeated)* Jools, do you think we could, do you mind if we... I think I might be done here now. Can we... you know... get on. Go our separate ways and all that.

JULIET Okay.

ALEX Okay.

*But **JULIET**, having seemed eager to get finished all along... suddenly doesn't want to go.*

JULIET So. That's yours, this is mine.

ALEX Yeah.

JULIET Okay, *(mind whirring)* could you just... move the bed bits into the hall? Don't want to, ahm, chip my nails.

ALEX Okay.

***ALEX** drags the heavy bedstead across the floor and out the door. **JULIET** instantly springs over to the briefcase and pops open the locks. The contents amaze her.*

JULIET *(whisper)* Jesus-Mary-Joseph-and-all-the-saints!!!

> *She finds the key and instantly turns to the locked sea chest. She slides the key into one of its three key holes. The kitchen door opens.*

ALEX What are you doing?

JULIET You've had a key all along.

ALEX What?

JULIET To this trunk… *(suddenly high pitched and flustered)* It's full of drugs isn't it? Cocaine and heroin and crystal dust.

ALEX Meth.

JULIET What?

ALEX Crystal meth. Not crystal dust. You're thinking of Angel Dust perhaps.

JULIET Oh. My. God. You are a drugs dealer! I KNEW you couldn't be that boring really.

ALEX Thanks. Thanks for that.

JULIET *(struggling)* Why won't the bloody thing open??

ALEX It's a very old lid locking system. 17th century. You have to put it in each of the three holes in turn. Left to right.

JULIET You lying bastard. You said you couldn't open it.
ALEX Well, to be precise, I said "You couldn't open it".

JULIET I thought you meant "one" can't open it. And you

know I thought that, you Sopranos-type character.

ALEX *(calm)* What on earth makes you think I'm a drug dealer Juliet?

JULIET The money! All that money! The lampstand gave you thousands, no, hundreds of thousands in used readies!

ALEX Don't try to do 'gangsta' sweetheart, you really can't carry it off.

JULIET Shut up you drug-dealing drug dealer!

She continues to try and open the chest.

ALEX You're going right to left. You need to go left to right.

JULIET Ha! Proud of your little stash are you? Drugs ruin lives you know! Trafficking and, and, and wassername, that poor Eastenders lady whose nose fell out and... oh.

There's a creak as the old chest gives up its secrets.

JULIET You were right. Left to right.

Another pause.

JULIET It's full of crap.

ALEX Not crack then?

JULIET No. Crap. More carefully filed crap. Theatre stubs and napkins and scrunchies and, ooh there's my contact lens box! I always wondered where... *(a pause)*

ALEX You got your eyes lasered so...

JULIET This is all my stuff.

Some rummaging.

JULIET That's my old driving licence. My old passport. *(fondly)* There's my windy-day-hat from Seattle.

More rummaging but more gentle this time.

JULIET *(confused)* It's the museum of me.

ALEX Kind of.

(numb)

JULIET You collected me.

ALEX Just things you didn't need anymore. Things you didn't miss.

JULIET My cashmere bedsocks my Mum knitted.

ALEX We got central heating. You threw them away 'cos of the holes. I just thought…

JULIET After they'd gone I really wished I hadn't.

JULIET And here are the… *(breaking up a little)* baby grows. And the little boots.

ALEX You asked me to take them to Oxfam but… I couldn't.

JULIET You collected me. Too.

ALEX Yes. Kind of.

JULIET Then I left you and you turned to drug dealing?

ALEX I am not a dealer of drugs. No plans to start either.

JULIET But you've got a briefcase with a million pounds in it.

ALEX A hundred and fifty seven thousand pounds in fact.

JULIET Are you a hit man? You were always very good with a pop gun at the fair.

ALEX I'm not a hit man Jools.

JULIET But a woman who looks like Gwyneth Paltrow's scrawnier sister gave you £157,000 in cash.

ALEX I sold my collections.

JULIET Well that's probably for the best but how did you get all this money?

ALEX I sold my collections.

JULIET WHAT???

ALEX I sold them. All of them. And... they came to £157,000.

JULIET Don't be ridiculous. McDonald's toys!? Spaceman scribbles?! Action men 1967 to the present day!?!

ALEX It's all to do with having complete sets. Neil Armstrong stopped signing 20 years before he died. His signature alone is worth £2,000. If you are the kind of person who wants all 12...

JULIET No person wants that!

ALEX ... Then the only way to get them is from someone like me who... started early.

JULIET But £157,000! For some crap in frames!

ALEX Yeah, that's how they are describing it in
the catalogue.

JULIET She's an auctioneer? Miss belt-instead-of-a-skirt?

ALEX Yes.

JULIET But why?

ALEX *(grin)* Well, I think the pay is good and you get a
free hammer.

JULIET No. I mean why did you sell them? You love your
crap. You're a crap collector. That's what you do.

ALEX I thought if I got rid of them it would help. But…

JULIET But?

ALEX Turns out… it didn't. It seems.

JULIET Help with what?

> *There's a long pause. Massive in fact.* **JULIET**'s *mind
> clearly whirring, knowing the answer to her own
> question but not quite knowing how she feels about it.*

ALEX Part of me thought… wished maybe… that you
didn't really want to go. Part of me hoped that you just
wanted me to… change.

JULIET *(gentle)* I'm not leaving you because of money Al.
You know that, don't you?

ALEX I do. I didn't mean that. Change as in… grow up.
Move on. Be a different kind of man. The money was a…
side effect.

JULIET Big side effect.

ALEX Then I realised that I did need a bit of money for something.

JULIET A bit?? A lot you mean.

ALEX No.

JULIET No?

ALEX No. It's only just enough in fact.

JULIET What for?

ALEX To catch a plane, then a train, then a boat.

JULIET *(already sort of knowing)* Where?

ALEX To a house. A house I need to buy. By a sea. Where there's nothing to do but eat fish, relax and maybe make a baby.

　　The longest pause of all.

ALEX I used to think I was not the sort of person you should replicate. That the world didn't need any more people who like things ordered and alphabetised and preferably laminated. But now I don't. Now I want to go to an island far away and make a baby.

JULIET Oh. Can you make a baby on your own?

ALEX It would certainly increase the chances if you came too.

JULIET Not by much.

ALEX You're wrong. You just need… the right conditions. Sun. Sea. Fish. No work. No Hugos. Then a baby… will come. A beautiful, messy, noisy, chaotic baby. *(Long pause)* I know we will be happy and a baby will come. And stay this time.

JULIET Just one?

ALEX Oh. Er. Well, I hadn't really… how many did you…?

JULIET I think that, after I've gone outside and had an embarrassing conversation with… I think that I might like to come with you. And maybe start a… collection.

They embrace and we're all done…

The End.

Property Plot

ACT ONE

Kettle

Toaster

Working gas hob

Working tap

Picture rail

Coffee

Tea

Sugar

Teaspoon

Mugs

Cardboard packing boxes (p1)

Box of pans (p1)

McDonald's Happy Meal (p1)

Large, late 90s mobile phone (p2)

Wind-up, small, green stegosauraus toy in wrapper (p3)

Bucket of water with mop (p4)

Wooden type case - each little box in the case has a colourful cheap toy carefully displayed in it. There are dozens of similar cases inside(p5)

Le Creuset cast-iron frying pan (p13)

Half a loaf of ciabatta bread (p15)

Chilli oil (p15)

Eggs (p15)

Cheese (p16)

Phone in the hall (p20)

Neatly mounted frame of 1930s American Baseball Cards (p22)

Long black glass-fronted box full of Japanese tin robots (p22)

Pinned and labelled insects (p22)

A complete set of Coke and Pepsi bottle caps, 1890s to the present day (p22)
Box full of random possessions (p33)
'Remember to get milk' chalk board and chalks (p34)
Pink furry handcuffs (p34)
Basque (p35)
Framed collections (p41)

Costume
Alex: Lumberjack shirt, white vest (p22)
Juliet: White, tight-fitting vest, cargo shorts (p41)

ACT TWO

Both actors shoud have a set of door keys

Large, lumpy objects under a white dust street (p47)
Bubble wrap (p52)
Under the dust sheet:
    A locked sea chest
    An old tandem
    A bedstead 'a french bed'
    A taxidermy puppy - (misshapen sausage dog)
    A print
    A bowl full of pebbles
    Entwining candle sticks
    Tin chicken that lays eggs 'it gives a squawk and plops out a tiny egg' (p53)
Two bags (p61)
UHT milk pots (p61)
Teapot (p67)

Costume
Alex: Thick coat (p47)
Juliet: Winter coat (p47)

Sound Effects Plot

ACT ONE

Front door opening (p1)
Waste disposal (p7)
Doorbell (p23)
Car door (p23)
Car pulling away (p29)
Door (p33)

ACT TWO

Door (p47)
Doorbell (p62)
Car (p76)
Door (p85)

Door opening and closing sound effects as needed.
Cars/van arriving/departing as needed.

Lighting Plot

ACT ONE

Lights up (p1)
Blackout (p46)

ACT TWO

Lights up (p47)
Blackout (p93)

Lightning Source UK Ltd.
Milton Keynes UK
UKOW06f0752040615

252882UK00001B/4/P